TANCHO

TANCHO

Poems

J. David Cummings

THE ASHLAND POETRY PRESS

Printed in the United States of America

ISBN: 978-0-912592-78-7

Library of Congress Control Number: 2014939250

Cover concept: J. David Cummings

Cover art: "Yosuke Yamahata," August 10, 1945, Nagasaki.
    Copyright © Shogo Yamahata/Courtesy: IDG films.

Cover design: Nicholas Fedorchak

Acknowledgements

A version of "Hiroshima Haibun" (10 poems) was a finalist in the Slapering
   Hol 2009 chapbook contest.
"Sadako-san" was published in the Slapering Hol Newsletter, April 2010
   edition.
"Tancho," "Folding the First Crane," and "A-bomb Dome" won honorable
   mention and were published in the Winning Writers War Poetry Con-
   test 2010.

*

I wish to express my deep gratitude to Alicia Ostriker, who selected this
work for the Richard Snyder Prize, and to the Ashland Poetry Press, espe-
cially to Deborah Fleming, Editor, and Sarah M. Wells, Managing Editor,
for their help and support in bringing *Tancho* to publication.

I also wish to thank Mr. Shogo Yamahata who kindly granted permis-
sion to use the torii photograph taken by his father, Mr. Yosuke Yamahata.
This photograph, which appears as part of the cover art of this book, along
with many others taken the day after the atomic bombing of Nagasaki, can
be found in the book *Nagasaki Journey: the Photographs of Yosuke Yamahata,
August 10, 1945* (Pomegranate Artbooks, San Francisco, 1995). The poems
appearing in the first section of *Tancho* are based on those photographs. I
cannot adequately express my appreciation for the courageous work car-
ried out by the senior Yamahata-san nor his son's generosity.

I further want to acknowledge the Waverley Writers Group of Palo
Alto, CA, which meets monthly. Earlier versions of these poems were read
there, beginning in the late nineties. Also, special thanks to Ann Chambers
(often my first reader) for her long standing interest and encouragement.

And finally, my sincere appreciation for the countless discussions I've
had over the years with Elizabeth Biller Chapman, Shirley Gaines, and
especially my wife, Christine Cummings, concerning all the poems appear-
ing here. Their help in shaping and improving the work has been invaluable.

for our children

Contents

IV. Messenger

I.

FORGOTTEN CITY

Torii, Nagasaki, August 10, 1945

The torii at the zero point
framing a membrane of gray light, a space
living in the enigma of time, to the eye
exactly like the space outside the gate, but not.
Because you can imagine it, enter and leave
in one motion, slip the tissue of the world,
and not know in which direction you have traveled.
It stands among a sea of broken things.
The Shinto shrine, gone. The maze of streets, gone.
The garden, the garden path, gone. The trees, gone.
All's below, beneath the ruptures of gray surface,
deep in the currents of the drowned and eaten.
And through the torii, a little distance in,
the stripped spine of the last tree, or the first.

Nagasaki Journey, Sergeant Yamahata-san's Last Assignment

The lens has done what it always does:
it has stopped the moment, made a door
in time.

      Twenty-eight when he walked through
all of it, the rubble underfoot, everywhere,
often stumbling, steadying the camera again.
All day the smoke and dust threading his lungs, all day
the corpses, the city's new nomads, stunned, wandering,
the blank expressions.

           At forty-eight he was dead of cancer.

Yamahata-san has said the camera brings stark fact
without the least need for embellishment.
The photographs are black and white.

It is as if one must indenture oneself,
the long passage to be worked off.
How did he persevere?

         A soldier's duty, of course.
The obligation to bear true witness, the absolute resolve,
the pitiless lens, honor.

He knew none of this about himself, haunted
by what seemed the coldness in his mind that day.

      Paper crane, charcoal green
    resting on an open page—
        things of emptiness.

Before the Hour

The houses face a soft morning light.
A hillside neighborhood. Wood-shingled roofs
climb the steep rise, packed so close together
the stone-paved streets can only be guessed
by tracking the zig-zag path of wired poles.
At the base of the hill, a small walking bridge,
a vague figure crossing below a white sky.

Are there always such mornings?

City Without Refuge

And then the hour, the devastation,
and the settling aftermath spreads out
in all directions of leveled ground, reaching
the half-ring of gray hills and distant mountains.

It was a small city; this must have been its heart.

Easy to imagine the houses, inns, shops, factories,
the vegetable gardens and marketplace,
people going about their morning business,
children setting out for school,
the ancient shrine... where now there's only
charred wood and white ash, broken tile, stone,
tortured iron: hard to tell what things are,
the white ash too thick and widely spread,
like a blanket of new-fallen snow, deceiving
the survivor's eye—

and corpses,
and the wandering *muga-muchu*—

a few smoke stacks, dark
totems of the new time;
in the middle distance,
the heaped remains of a factory
like a black tumor.

Two Travelers Starting Out

These are the first faces.
Let me believe they are brother and sister.

Sacks and suitcases loading them down,
a rolled blanket pinched under an arm,
the two seem stopped for his camera—

more likely they're only catching their breath,
or pausing to plan the next uncharted step...

The boy is younger, teenaged,
his face is turned partially away;
he is looking toward the ground
at something behind his sister.
Impossible to know what's
catching his eye. Perhaps a useful
object, not quite buried
beneath the ash and splintered wood.
Or he's averting his eyes,
not wanting the camera to learn
what has been taken. Or he's noticed
six soldiers a few feet away, three on a side,
carrying a body on a stretcher.

Not the young woman, she has not turned
from the camera. She looks past it,
a level gaze, her mouth slightly open.
You can't see her eyes, only dark
crescent shapes, high cheekbones
hiding whatever might have taken residence.

The face is unmarred, has the beauty of youth.
You can see intention there,
and strength.
                    Her left hand grips
a cloth bag, floral design, her right
a cheap suitcase, and a strap crosses
her chest from right shoulder to hip, the sack
supported on her left buttock; across
her shoulder blades, another sack, a netting
of some sort that is knotted at the sternum,
which pins her arms straight to her sides, the bag
and suitcase scraping against her legs.
She stands firmly planted. She is twenty. Gray blouse,
rolled sleeves, long black skirt with a flower print,
perhaps the early bulge of pregnancy.

                    A crane of pale rose,
            a small creature, well-folded—
                    the soul bowing.

The Corpse of a Very Young Child

Just a thing among the rubble ocean
of shattered wood, tile shards, twisted iron...

The legs are black and rigid. The left one
is level, almost straight, stabbing
the air a foot or so above the ground;
the right, bent forward at the hip
and bent again at the knee: as if the legs
were caught running, in mid-stride, and
frozen in the fire; as if the body were
a stone cherub blown from its pedestal
and violently tumbled, coming to rest
against the trunk of a toppled tree.

But here's a simpler reading:
fixed in the photograph is the child's death spasm.
The little boy or girl (the genitals
too charred to know which) has been there,
on the ruined ground hour after hour,
knowing only molten pain—

the left leg thrusts straight out, the head
twists right at the same time jerking back
as if trying to rise up, the burned face
turning, pitching into the dirt,
and the last breath breathes in the dust,
the last cry is given to the earth.

Words

Kyoku Kaneyama-san wrote this soon after the bombing:

> The flash that covered
> the city in morning mist—
> an instant dream.

And Yamahata-san would reflect years later about the cold night air, the sky overflowing with stars, and so many small fires—elf fires—rising from the smoldering bodies. He would say then how strangely beautiful the scene his camera could not see, what only words might find. What one hibakusha's tanka recalled of the ice-black nights of August ninth and tenth:

> blue phosphorescent
> flames rising from the dead
> as spirits rose
> in former days—fireballs,
> tradition's name.

I want the eye of my mind to linger on the scene it has never seen. I want to concede the universality of Beauty there in the pitch black, the scatter of blue fires among hillock and gully and field, lighting the way. I would see it, the great spectrum of sorrow, the loneliness of flame. Such quiet in the blue motion, the whispering nothing.

So I write for them, for us

> the strangest of flames
> flickering in the stillness—
> this new way of death.

Were He a Boy, Sleeping

At first you don't see him,
and you don't see the slender trees outside,
the close-in brush, the overturned wood crates
buried in the wide rectangle of afternoon light—
too bright a brilliance, sharpened
in the black frame of house timbers,
all of it defining a passage not there before.

But gradually your eye adjusts, the glare softens,
and you begin to make out interior shapes:
intact cedar beams, the remnants
of a sliding door, a slight clutter of debris...
you see him last.
                        He lies flat
on his stomach, head turned from the light,
the side of his face resting on the floor,
left arm bent just in front, and his bare legs
stretched out straight, feet in extension,
the tops of his toes touching wood, pointed
perfectly, like one diving into water. He seems
a youth of ten or eleven. He seems to be sleeping,
and the light dapples him.

        There are butterflies
    warming in broken sunlight—
        wake up, child, wake up.

Hibakusha

People are walking through.
I think no more than a dozen
　　can be counted. Nearly all are
walking out, field of white ruins
　　growing larger as they arrive
where they had lived another life.
　　And if you could see that far in,
then blank eyes and empty faces.
　　But three are going back, into
first loss, seeking their loved ones gone
　　in the white flash, the open mouth
of the sky, which had received all
　　that had been the summer morning.

One man in particular:
who is new to the photograph,
who wears a clean white shirt,
who has an undamaged bicycle,
who is entering from the right,
who carries nothing,
who is walking back in
from the day before the day before
or from twenty thousand days to come.

Young Woman Among Rubble: Day Scene

You see her, and you cannot believe what you see.
Not because this open charnel, its charred remains
scattered about like so many burnt logs, assaults the eye,
and not because you see survivor after survivor,
dazed, devoid of self, wandering rubble streets,
hour into hour into nightfall,
but because the young woman is like an oasis,
    something incomprehensible
        half-emerged from underground—
the shelter not unlike a root cellar; her clothes
are impeccable, her hands delicate and clean
even as they touch the dirt walls to steady
her ascent from earthed safety.
                      She seems new.
The end of winter: black coat, gray silk scarf
tied around her hair, wisp of hair brushing forehead,
her face a lovely symmetry, unblemished skin,
a muted yellow-ivory, and she is smiling
that gracious smile one offers an honored guest.

Nagasaki Afternoon

It is the afternoon of August 10th—
you can tell by the light, the angle of the shadows.
The nurses and doctors have arrived. They have begun
their ministrations. They have nothing
for what confronts them, but of course they do
what they can.
     The burns are something
they think they know, yet they have only
rapeseed oil, which gives a white, other-worldly
shine when they smooth it on a back, a chest, limbs...
and tincture of iodine.
       They go
from clump to clump of ruined human beings,
   men and women and children
who hardly move, hardly speak, who seem to be
looking into something in the near distance
that their fixed eyes alone can see.
       Sitting
in a cart, on straw, a mother
is trying to breast-feed her two-year-old.
Her robe is open, the warm Nagasaki sun
bathes her collarbone and small breast.
         Unmarred.
Her skin, except for a bruise and cut on her cheek,
has still the smoothness of her years, her hair
is shiny, parted down the center of her head,
pulled back in a bun, black.
   Her burns are buried, beyond the eye.

And the child at her breast does not suckle. Perhaps
it is only tired. Perhaps the spider web of burn marks
on the face and head are superficial,
and the bruising of left forearm and hand slight,
because the skin of the shoulder and side and belly and legs,
the curled fingers (that hold tight the opened robe)
are as smooth and clear, as warmed in the sunlight
as the mother's warm skin.
                              But it will not suckle.
            Then a doctor
comes by, leans over them, lightly applies a little
ointment to the baby's head, and the baby begins fussing.
Soon the doctor leaves, sunlight replaces him.
The baby falls off to sleep, the nipple held loosely
in its still mouth.

        And the mother looks
        into that shallow distance
          a few feet from them,
        seeing, I suppose, nothing—
        but what is in her face, what?

II.

HIROSHIMA HAIBUN

Koji-san

Koji-san is hibakusha nisei.
His mother lived in Hiroshima
when she was a girl, and that morning
she was down in the root cellar, fetching
something for her mother, dallying,
when the Bomb exploded above their heads,
turning the August morning sky into fire
and sealing her in a terrible darkness
for three days, her mother gone. She was six,
about my age then.

                          I was surprised
he told me any of this. I hadn't asked.
We were having lunch, engaged in small talk,
relaxing a bit after our visit
to Ryoan-ji Temple at the far end
of the city, two bus rides away.
He'd been showing me Kyoto on a rainy
Saturday, the cherry blossoms beginning.
Some time during the morning I'd asked him
if it was hard to get to Hiroshima
from Osaka. "No, you take the Bullet Train,"
he said. "It's just few hours ride." He would
meet me at the train station on Monday,
help me buy a ticket, but not go himself.

                          I think my question
was unexpected. From time to time,
he gave me a puzzled look. Yet he would not
allow himself to break the privacy.
I could not have explained.

Bullet Train

What leads to what is more often than not uncanny,
as if fate itself were unlikely but still fate;
or taking the Bullet Train to Hiroshima
from Osaka, alone, an early April morning,
derived like theorem and proof from the ten years
spent as a weapons worker. A physicist, one
of those seekers after the secrets of the garden
where grows the nuclear flower, but one who had no
passion for the work and left it. Not that some clear day
came calling, telling me to leave the Livermore Lab
straight away, the morning's new yield of arcane numbers
abandoned in panic, a fit of shame or hope.
No, the way out was a labyrinth of false purpose;
yet every step, every turn could lead only here.

      Under way in morning
    light, pink blossoms streaking by—
       no companion.

Mount Fuji

> All year round
> Fuji-no-yama—who sees
> Hokusai's old world?

I was hoping to glimpse Mount Fuji from the train,
but coming out, there were so many close-in hills.
Watchful Fuji-san seemed a far way from Osaka,
and I was heading opposite.
                              Past this station there is,
perhaps, no clear line of sight leading back, though the train
hurtles toward its appointment in Hiroshima.

Not once while it rocketed south and west
did I think of my time with the weapons. (How
is it done, this keeping the self from itself?)
I was instead taken with watching an alien,
sun-flooded landscape streak by.
                              But not alien.
The forested low mountains, the small farms, the fat wires
dipping, flying alongside—Pennsylvania country
fifty years ago. And these hills too came so near, the light fled.

> Black cables swoop and rise,
> wooded hills close, then through a notch
> Fuji's white hat!

Aioi Street in Shadow

It's a long walk from Hiroshima Station
down Aioi Street to Peace Memorial Park.
The street is now a modern thoroughfare, showing
nothing of its past. But in the walk there is time
for losing the sightseer's safe interests,
for letting in what happened here, to be no more
the self-assured American not remembering
the scientist's bomb, the samurai's great sword, two flags
that burned four years in hell. Even the city's miracle—
that forest of buildings, storefronts, overhead wires,
the sidewalk crowds hurrying toward their intentions,
the wide, stenchy flood of vehicles—none of it
could keep me from the black ash.... No one looked at me
as I walked between them. What was it I must feel?
     Then I came to the first bridge of the perished
     and watched a long time the water flowing.

          Bridge with a human
     shadow flashed into stone—who
          watches me pass today?

          Wing shadow on water—
     in this reborn city
          no one travels alone.

          On water, rippled
     whispers, shadows moving through—
          deep home, homeless.

A-bomb Dome

Coming on it from the northeast on this early spring
afternoon, it is all in soft shadow. Dark but not
brooding dark. Yet a brooding settles on the ragged shape,
the open dome of twisted girders like wrought filigree,
its interior sky a blue quilt of tortured forms,
and its blown-out windows like notches a razor-light
had cut into flesh——because one knows what it is,
what it means. *Because one knows.* Therefore ominous,
this afternoon darkness, as if the frame of human time
stood revealed. But then, when you circle to its sunlit side,
it seems a harmless thing. No more than a worn and broken
structure empty of its life, its voices, its industry:
shell of brick and concrete half-walls wanting to fall,
wanting winter's next increment of work...
                    but holding fast.

As for A-bomb Dome—
samurai's battered armor,
    empty-headed helmet.

As for A-bomb Dome—
in the helmet's sky-blank eyes
    no view of Fuji.

As for A-bomb Dome—
old warrior's shoulder bones
    warming in the sun.

As for A-bomb Dome—
silent walls in still decay,
    acknowledgments of spring.

As for A-bomb Dome—
Buddha and the Bodhi tree,
    and us, this ruin?

As for A-bomb Dome—
for August sixth, six haiku:
    the cicada's shell.

You would feel a troubling as you stood before it
in the warm April air. You would feel the familiarity,
the strangeness as one. Here is the incomprehensible,
what we have known from a hundred photographs,
here before us, silent, fragile, unfamiliar at last.
Try saying to yourself "like Roman ruins." Try thinking
"just the past's leftovers," as if that could free us from it.
Unbroken line threading through wars lost in time
and wars celebrated in song and story,
through flash-boom and black rain, through the eye
of this moment, through the next, and the next—
no safe harbor, no ocean of time to separate
first horror from last, victim from victim.
Now a new gene, white-fire forged, a stealth at work,
counting down, cell by cell, our lives. Here hibakusha.
           I bow. I bow to them who refused erasure.
           I bow before this confounding human nature.

Peace Memorial Park

Then I crossed Aichi Bridge and entered the park,
and it seemed that I had entered a state of grace.
No, I didn't see descending flaming emerald wings
or the Ghost's white tongues of fire. I saw children.
I saw them under cherry blossom, evergreen
and bare branch, under sunlight and brilliant blue.
I saw mothers and fathers, grandparents: love's attending.

                 Here too I moved invisible
and was deeply glad for it, that I would disturb
no thing nor any child. —As if an unseen angel
had swept my spirit into a future I'd believed lost
or lent me an afternoon's vision that I might rejoice in
this innocence, these small bodies, these newborn souls.

          Surprise, surprise—
            how like the blossoms these children!
            had I never seen spring?

Cenotaph

So I thought it could be enough just to walk the park,
to keep outdoors and let the day unfold. What need
did I have for guidebook or audio tape, the museum's
grim displays? I would go where my eyes led, toward
what hearing desired. In the things I saw, the sounds
that came, the monuments and children, I might learn
as much as I can know of psalm and counterpoint,
hope and despair, the promise of each to the other.

In alignment the tomb rhymes north to the A-bomb Dome,
a lodestone shell guiding sorrow's eye to its polar star;
but intervening, there is also a reflecting pool
and a low, wide-winged stone structure at its northern reach,
and a timeless flame placed at the centerline of that rhyme:
flame and wing floating over water, under the Dome's watch.

      Hollow house of souls—
   the mortal eye sees straight through,
     all the way to Doom.

Children's Peace Monument

                              I don't recall exactly when
the bell's sound came to me. It drifted on the air:
sound then silence then sound again then long silence,
as if everywhere. I began to desire it,
to seek for it, but soon ten thousand folded cranes
broke in, cranes strung tight together in garlands
of color, high hanging or in heaps, in fine disorder,
a vibrant profusion, like mountain wildflowers
carpeting a cool upland meadow in August.

—I knew this place already, knew her story, her cranes.
Now, Sadako-san's statue stands at the heights,
facing a wanting world, her new body firm of limb,
arms uplifted, fingers like wing tips crafting the air,
all in a rhyme with the crane that crowns her, that brought her here,
that carries every infirm child up the fabled mountain.

And on the memorial stone:

> *"This is our cry,*
> *This is our prayer,*
> *For building peace in the world."*

Peace Bell

Again the bell. Dark solemn sound, deep and river broad.
At first, it seemed only a single note, but then
a higher tone in small delay emerging,
and the two setting up a softly ringing, slow vibrato.
Harmony in the slight disharmony, a woven sound
that reached out like a call to prayer. And dying out,
the silence flowing in, the silence insisting,
you wouldn't want any longer to believe in death
but wouldn't know if you could believe in prayer.
Yet prayer would enter and wordless you would pray:
not for this world, but for the world the children travel to—
these children, your children, the children of your enemy.

> Listen, little cricket,
> that slow tolling—the bell,
> why is it still hiding?

It puzzled me, that evanescent ringing.
Such a pious sound, struck at any moment
like an offhand Angelus, the day not arrived
at some well-known hour of sacred ceremony.
But once I'd walked through the small congress of trees,
past Sadako-san's station, the bell took its form.
It hung in the center of a round pavilion,
a large black chrysalis, unattended and silent
like the darkest of questions—

> which only the park's children could answer:
> for they would run up to it,

pause a moment, then one by one would ring it,
while the rest stood quietly, wrapped in the bell's great sound.
  I remember my aha! and my delight;
  here they were: playing, doing the work of priests.

Sadako-san

But recently I found a black and white photograph.
She is twelve, a single figure standing in a whiteness.
It is her last year, and I do not know the occasion,
though it has weight, for she is wearing her finest kimono.
Even in this old recovered photograph, the silk shines.
She seems wrapped in it, secured, her arms arrested,
slender wrists bare below the sleeves. And her hands—
hands soon to fold nine hundred sixty-four cranes—so still.
Yet it is her small, round face that haunts me. How serious
she is, those dark eyes looking out at me forever
from that place of forever, something passing through the veil,
something of what winter's beauty is. And behind her
new houses, leafless trees, a ditch, rebuilt Hiroshima.
There is no child but this child.

> Sadako-san, somber unfinished child of cranes,
> dead October 25, 1955—
> ten years and eighty-one days after the black rains.

Who, on any day, looking up at the park's brave statue
or down at a new offering of cranes, would not embrace
the ease of hope? But in this recovered face, this child
of eternity, is as true a form. Let me hold her
constant in thought that the work of hope work water and rock.

> Light of two Sadako-san to guide me,
> one in stone imagined, one real;
> one the rare light of joy, one sorrow's light—
> let each call to me the other.

Hibakusha

There is in the park a burial mound
that houses the ashes of the unknown dead
and a stone coffin meant to hold the names
of those whose ashes roiled in the atom storm
and flew with the winds to the far corners
of this blue pearl. But those who have lived on
in the ruin of their bodies, that name
a shaming whisper, where is their monument?

If hibakusha are turned away, isn't
the past lost to us? And the present, what is
the present then but a child's forgetfulness?

I would remember them, honor their true name.
And remembering, would we be spared the black rains?
Impossible to say. But this forgetting, no.

On a small stone is written
"... we shall not repeat this evil."

The Gift of Memory and Forgetting

Looking back all these years later, how easy
to remember the gift: the children of the park,
playing at their invented games, the bounty
of paper cranes, those colors indeed a music,
and the bell's deep sounding that led me
from station to station, as if I were
once more in the church of my childhood,
and too the savvy pigeons, chased and lifting,
just out of reach of the smallest ones
still a bit unsteady as they run,
and their parents gathering them in
for picture taking, smoothing those bright energies
for that moment of stilled time, then
letting them go again.

                    —Why remember grief,
what can it redeem?

                    *

I came to believe in a fierce remembering,
thinking that if hibakusha were invited
into the mind each day and seen as they are—
          scar and anguished soul and us—
then, I thought, every obscenity of war
would come flooding in and for a day,
          that day, war would die.

In time, I perceived the error: to live
so deep in the past, August sixth cast
across the waking hours, hibakusha dreams
defining the night, our children bent
to those sorrows,
                    the present, the future stolen—
there's no healing there, no safety.

                    *

Year after year, word by word
Hiroshima evaporated into the silence.
People got on with their lives, children dreamed,
and I thought, This is how it happens.
All the words of remorse and remembrance,
the scream that lies beneath,
will have no suasion.

I want for some other way of memory,
one that holds a bit of forgetting, a bit of hope.

I suppose the Park is a good remembering, the bell is,
                    each year the offered poem—
never enough, Koji-san, never…

                    *

                    The bell stands silent—
                in the grass crickets quiet—
                    summer evening, late.

III.

AN IMPLICATE WORLD

Folding the First Crane

at the start, a sweet awkwardness
this prayer of peace so new
though already it moves
within the compass of my hands
how can I say it? as if I
could never fold this little
messenger into being
as if I had never stopped—

first: an uncreased square, color side up
a shape seldom found perfect in Nature
valley folded along diagonals
two triangles appear and disappear
the square reopened, turned over, folded
east, unfolded, folded north, unfolded
two rectangles of hue come and go—

three primal forms the eye perceives inside
the true world of forms, vain inventions
there and not there yet form at the very
heart of that old worn dream of mastery
(only the circle will make no showing)
and so the error of the ideal world comes
calling, the world of lifted-out perfection
overarching and there follows geometry
and number, science, philosophy, and sword
there follows the beauty wrought by human hands—

as with this small abstract creature forming
in the two worlds simultaneously
as with it unfolded for the last time
the four corners brought one by one together
the color square reappearing, half its size
and with flaps right and left, top and bottom
primal form same and altered, evolved
more useful now to complex intention—

second: folds and forms explicate
symmetries abound, turn, reverse, or break
the many follows quickly on the one
the dream of the organic arises
shapes, seeming to live unseen inside each
other, fixed in some elsewhere existence
are coaxed by hand and thought to come through
themselves to me, revealing an implicate world
wherein it waits and in the paper foldings
only the simplest complexities show
but these are dazzling as they advance
toward the crane of peace so hidden here
I cannot yet imagine her—

but she is coming
through the frog's mouth as it opens wide
through the long diamond of the petal fold
through the corners freed and tapering into legs
through two transforming book folds
though still not petal into nascent crane, but fox
the fine face of the fox arrives

and she is in there, she is nearly
visible as fox's ears soon change
into shy wings, that long narrow nose
into tail and neck, and the neck's tip
reversing into head and pointed beak—

yet she will not come whole into this world
until I gently pull open the wings
and at the very last breathe
a warm slow breath into her body—

third: nothing less than this

                    *

birds—
we called them *birds*

they haven't flown (yet)
they sleep upright, silent in their silo roosts
they make safe your children the MAD have said
and

inside each bird a warhead
inside each warhead a design
inside each design a calculation
inside each calculation an algorithm
inside each algorithm an improvement
inside an improvement my name

which is how, years later, he put it, my old boss
at a Mozart concert intermission, running across
me in the lobby—of course the usual talk
of forgotten colleagues, of weather, of music—
then he says, our work worked out fine and by the way
he says, there's a Moscow nuke and *your* name's on it
and he barks a quick laugh, his eyes moist and shining,
and he eyes me sharply and I have no idea
what he sees I fear the worst
therefore...

therefore, I am become Death again
cold logic has it

and I make myself imagine it
the billions
by my mind's small hand
hurried into death

and if the unflown birds never fly
and if the myriad suns never light
and logic relents?

I make myself understand

my eternal name reversed, reversed again
unknown to me in all Time's passing

and your name
the shape of silence
and your voice
the form of silence

tell it now to me
tell the names we will carry into the earth

the cold light has shown the letters and the stones
and the veil is burning in clear ice
and no innocence is left

*

and the moment when the first crane came
into my world, and how, when I set
her down to stand wing-raised and silent
on the table, there seemed surrounding
her an egg of warm light and still air

and she was the most gentle being
I had ever seen, and how it seemed
pure moment, in which time had not yet
begun to act on her
                              was she not
soul itself just before the journey
light and form and vulnerability
caught in the fine steel net of the real
a seed set down in this soil
the very first of her kind?

and imperfect, she was perfect

and here—in this space, this time
not an apparition floating
beyond the reach of fingertips
but the smallest gesture
imaginable in the work
that awaits our faltering hands

this little bird of bright paper

hardly the sure occasion
of new beginnings yet no one
of this age of blood and ash and bone
can know which act seeds, which translates
which reverses the pitch of war...

IV.

MESSENGER

Grus japonensis

In Japan she is called tancho,
a word that means red crown and crane.
Her crown is more skull cap than crown,
but in the north sea island winter
dull red brightens at mating time,
and then she's the most graceful mistress
of the pas de deux. And she is
neither solitary nor many,
though time was she lived everywhere
among them, even as they warred.
Whatever struggle had been their lives,
they had always believed in her;
but then they lost their faith, and she
was hunted for her flesh and feathers.
The eating made them no less fierce;
the lavish feathers no more artful.
What had changed in them that they should
exchange the dream of peace for gain,
these malign one hundred years since?

Tancho

As when five years after, in the brutal winter
of nineteen-fifty, their numbers down
to the twenty-five hunched low like white stone loaves
around a hot spring and the three that have strayed
onto the wind-cut snowfields, pecking hard
the ice-crusted futility: these red crowned cranes,
starved out, unsheltered, their kind hunted
down into death by falconer and farmer
in a mere one hundred years, here in this last place
of snowscape and volcano, bitter north sea island
so seeming far from the blast and scorch of war;
and too weak now to bring the message the gods
have uttered, and too weak to lift aloft
our rag souls toward the Western Paradise...

As when he returned to them, emerging
out of a line of spruce like a lone gray
apparition, and not empty-handed
this time, refusing this time the severing,
though seeing them I doubt he thought the ancient names—
"emissary," "carrier of souls," "bearer
of good fortune, long life"; yet his charity
was remembrance as he fetched out the grain
the worn sack concealed and began tossing
to them their new life, began seeding it.
A single farmer, standing alone somewhere
near the edge of the great Kushiro Marsh,
the Akan at his back, Hokkaido
winter in his bones. What possessed him?

small sanctuary
tucked deep away
on an island of brief summers
and faithful winters—

how few were the hands
that brought them refuge
and how few these few
hundred breeding pairs
and saved, they are not safe.

*

This is not the Isle of the Blessed
and that is not the absolute white.
Crowned head, bright red, black neck scarf and face,
blond bill, bustle of velvet black plumes,
and white snow the breast and wings and back:
they put to the air, a graceful lift
of large bodies, line of spruce falling
away, winter blue ocean of sky
washing over them as they form up
their flight, loudly calling as they go—
telling you this is the real,
singing the great impossible,
telling you everything.

A bell sounding peace,
the wheel of snow wings, turning
the light toward us.

Notes

These notes provide background information for some of the poems found in this book, as well as definitions for a number of Japanese words appearing in the texts of the poems.

I. Forgotten City

"Torii": The Japanese word *torii* refers to a gateway structure consisting of two uprights with a straight crosspiece at the top and a concave lintel above the crosspiece. It is usually made of wood (often painted vermilion) or stone and is commonly built at the approach to a Shinto shrine but can be seen in other locations throughout Japan. A torii defines an open space; there is no gate attached to the uprights that might bar entry or exit.

"City Without Refuge": The Japanese word *muga-muchu* refers to the survivors of the atomic bombings at Hiroshima and Nagasaki. After the attacks, muga-muchu wandered the city streets in silence or sat motionless in the rubble, lost in a profound daze. The term suggests a person who is without a self or center to his/her being, as if dead though alive.

"Words": The haiku and tanka in this poem are based on remarks made by the writer Kyoku Kaneyama, quoted in *Nagasaki Journey: The Photographs of Yosuke Yamahata, August 10, 1945*; Rupert Jenkins Editor; Pomegranate Art Books, San Francisco.

   The Japanese word *hibakusha* refers to a person or persons who survived the atomic bombing at Hiroshima or Nagasaki, and also to the descendants of these survivors.

II. Hiroshima Haibun

Haibun is a Japanese literary form that combines prose narrative and haiku. It usually relates a journey of some sort. The number of haiku appearing within the narrative is not fixed, but the haiku and narrative interact; each prepares the way for and amplifies the other. "Hiroshima Haibun" is an adaptation of this form into American English. Except for the poems "Koji-san" and "The Gift of Memory and Forgetting," I have used a greatly modified sonnet form instead of prose to carry the narrative and a somewhat loosened haiku form that I hope honors the spirit of the Japanese form.

Background of the Peace Memorial Park and Peace Festival

Hiroshima Peace Memorial Park has been built at ground zero of the atomic bomb explosion, on a small island between the Motoyau and Hon Rivers (part of the Ota River delta system). In the summer of 1949, the surviving people of Hiroshima voted for the construction of this park. Plans were drawn up and construction began the following year, with the completion and dedication of the first monument, the Cenotaph, taking place on August 6, 1952. Since then, construction and landscaping have continued on an ongoing basis. At the time of this writing, there are approximately sixty dedicated monuments within or next to the park. A number of these monuments have been contributed by organizations outside Japan.

The first peace festival, or public commemoration of the atomic bombing of Hiroshima, was held on August 6, 1947 at Jisenji-no-hana, which is an open area now included in the park and known as Peace Square. The ceremony that day was simple. It took place around a wooden clock tower that had been built for the occasion. At 8:15 a.m., the time of the explosion two years earlier, a silent prayer was observed and then the Peace Bell in the tower was rung. Following this, the Mayor of Hiroshima read aloud the first Peace Declaration, in which he called for a "revolution of thought," necessitated by the advent and use of atomic (nuclear) weapons.

From this modest beginning, the Peace Festival has become an annual international event. On the morning of August sixth, thousands of people from almost every country fill the park. The ceremonies have grown in number and complexity.

The day still begins at 8:15 a.m. with the ringing of the Peace Bell. (Bells also ring throughout Hiroshima at the same time.) One minute of silent prayer follows. Then a number of prayers and speeches are given, fresh flowers offered, and hundreds of white doves released. After this, groups carrying all sorts of peace banners march through the park, often pausing at various monuments to offer prayers. Anyone is free to join these marches. The day takes on the feel of a summer O-bon or Festival of the Dead.

One particularly notable event is the day-long "die-in" held at the Atomic Dome (A-bomb Dome). People lie down side by side, in close proximity, and remain quiet, feigning death, in memory of the victims of the first August sixth. This ceremony lasts into the night, with people participating as they wish. After dark, as a final attempt to console the spirits of the dead, paper lanterns are floated down the Ota River. Each lantern comprises a small paper sac with a lit votive candle placed in it and bears the name of someone who encountered the atomic bombing.

Poems

"Bullet Train": The "Livermore Lab" refers to the Lawrence Livermore National Laboratory in Livermore, California. It is one of the two national laboratories in the United States charged with the mission to research, develop, and maintain nuclear weapons.

"Mount Fuji": The lines "who sees/Hokusai's old world" refer to the artist Katsushika Hokusai and his famous paintings, "Thirty-six Views of Mount Fuji." The paintings depict ordinary 19th-century Japanese life as it was conducted under the "watchful eye" of Mount Fuji, which appears somewhere in each painting.

"A-bomb Dome": This badly damaged building was one of the very few structures left standing at ground zero after the atomic explosion, and is the only one that was not razed. Whether to save the structure as a reminder of that day of atomic devastation provoked controversy in Japan for two decades. Finally, in June 1966, a resolution to preserve the structure was passed. Before the war, the building served as the Hiroshima Prefectural Industrial Promotion Hall. Today it is known as the A-bomb Dome or Atomic Dome.

The term "flash-boom" is the descriptive English equivalent of the Japanese word *pikadon*, which refers to the actual experience of the atomic bomb explosion. For an explanation of "black rain," see the note on "Sadako-san" that follows.

As noted earlier, hibakusha refers to the survivors of the atomic bombings. The children and grandchildren of first generation hibakusha are known as hibakusha nisei and hibakusha sensei, respectively. Over the years, hibakusha have been marginalized in Japan. Fortunately, there have also been vigorous efforts to reverse this trend.

"Children's Peace Monument" and "Sadako-san": These two poems revolve around the Hiroshima schoolgirl Sadako Sasaki, who, apparently healthy, survived for ten years after the bombing and in whose memory the Children's Peace Monument was erected in 1958. Sadako-san is known around the world, especially among children, for attempting to fold 1000 origami cranes during her illness at age twelve. She believed that if she could fold 1000 paper cranes, health and good fortune would be hers again. At the time, many in Japan held this belief. Sadako-san managed to fold 964 cranes. Her friends and classmates folded the remaining thirty-six, and all 1000 cranes were buried with her.

Since her death, as a kind of prayer for peace and for a world free of nuclear weapons, the folding of paper cranes has been taken up by children and even adults all over the world. Tens of thousands of colorful paper cranes that have been strung into garlands are sent to the park each year. They can be seen throughout the park but especially at the Children's Peace Monument.

The monument consists of a 9-meter high, grayish-white concrete tripod base with a bronze statue of a twelve-year-old girl atop it. The girl's hands are raised above her head and hold a large, "folded" bronze crane. To either side of her, suspended midway up the base, are two children, a boy and a girl. Some regard the base of the monument as representing Mount Horai, the fabled mountain of the Western Paradise. Cranes are said to carry souls there. Thus, the little statue shows a triumphant Sadako-san crowned by a golden crane that has transported her to the Western Paradise, as the boy and girl joyfully rise up the great mountain.

The term "black rain" refers to the sooty, radioactive rain that fell intermittently throughout the day after the explosion. Many were exposed to this slow, silent killer, including Sadako-san and her family. Those who suffered with agonizing burns welcomed the cooling rain.

III. An Implicate World

The notion of an "implicate world" is taken from the book *Wholeness and the Implicate Order*, written by the physicist David Bohm. In this conception, the world as it appears to us constitutes an "explicate" or "unfolded" order, which derives from a deeper, "implicate" order, a wholeness normally hidden from us.

"Folding the First Crane": This poem explores David Bohm's ideas about explicating an implicate order through the steps of folding an origami crane.

MAD is an acronym for "mutually assured destruction." It was Cold War jargon for the strategic military concept of mutual nuclear deterrence between the Soviet Union and the United States. It assumed no entity in possession of nuclear weapons would be insane to the point of precipitating a nuclear exchange and thereby causing the annihilation of human civilization.

The line "therefore I am become Death again" references the lines "Now I am become Death/the Destroyer of worlds" from the *Bhagavad-Gita*. The physicist J. Robert Oppenheimer, who directed the Manhattan Project, said these lines came to him immediately after witnessing the successful test of the first atomic bomb at Trinity site in Alamogordo, New Mexico on July 16, 1945.

IV. Messenger

"Tancho": The Japanese word for the red crowned crane (*Grus japonensis*) is *tancho*. In the Japanese culture, tancho is a sacred bird. It is regarded as an omen of good fortune and was common throughout Japan before hunting restrictions were lifted in the late 19th century. Now, it is found in the wild only on the northernmost island of Hokkaido, where it is protected. The birds number in the hundreds at most and no longer migrate.

"North sea island" is another name for the island of Hokkaido.

The Kushiro Marsh is located on the eastern coast of Hokkaido. The Akan River flows through the crane sanctuary, which is situated within the marsh. The Akan is also the volcanic mountain readily visible from the marsh.

The Richard Snyder Publication Series

This book is the 17th in a series honoring the memory of Richard Snyder (1925-1986), poet, fiction writer, playwright and longtime professor of English at Ashland University. Snyder served for fifteen years as English Department chair and was co-founder (in 1969) and co-editor of the Ashland Poetry Press. He was also co-founder of the Creative Writing major at the school, one of the first on the undergraduate level in the country. In selecting the manuscript for this book, the editors kept in mind Snyder's tenacious dedication to craftsmanship and thematic integrity.

Deborah Fleming, Editor, selected finalists for the 2013 contest.
Final judge: Alicia Ostriker.

Snyder Award Winners:

1997: Wendy Battin for *Little Apocalypse*
1998: David Ray for *Demons in the Diner*
1999: Philip Brady for *Weal*
2000: Jan Lee Ande for *Instructions for Walking on Water*
2001: Corrinne Clegg Hales for *Separate Escapes*
2002: Carol Barrett for *Calling in the Bones*
2003: Vern Rutsala for *The Moment's Equation*
2004: Christine Gelineau for *Remorseless Loyalty*
2005: Benjamin S. Grossberg for *Underwater Lengths in a Single Breath*
2006: Lorna Knowles Blake for *Permanent Address*
2007: Helen Pruitt Wallace for *Shimming the Glass House*
2008: Marc J. Sheehan for *Vengeful Hymns*
2009: Jason Schneiderman for *Striking Surface*
2010: Mary Makofske for *Traction*
2011: Gabriel Spera for *The Rigid Body*
2012: Robin Davidson for *Luminous Other*
2013: J. David Cummings for *Tancho*